For Hilda

TIME REMEMBERED

TIME REMEMBERED
A Journal for Survivors

EARL A. GROLLMAN

BEACON PRESS   Boston

Beacon Press
25 Beacon Street
Boston, Massachusetts 02108

Beacon Press books are published under the auspices
of the Unitarian Universalist Association
of Congregations in North America.

Text and cover design by Rae Ann Grant
"Pimpernel" leaf pattern by William Morris used on front
panel by courtesy of the Board of Trustees of the Victoria
and Albert Museum

Contents

Introduction   1

GRIEVING
Who Am I?   5
The Faces of Death   8
    Shock
    Denial
    Guilt
    Anger
    Tears
    Physical Reactions
    Depression

WORKING THROUGH GRIEF
Practical Matters   43
Special Dates and Holidays   46
Children Need Help, Too   51

SUPPORT
Friends   57
Self-Help Groups   61
Helping Others   65
Religion   69

RECOVERY
Life Goes On   77

Growing Through Loss   81
Time Remembered   85
Endings and Beginnings   89

A Sanskrit Proverb   93
Afterword   95

APPENDIXES

For winter's rains and ruins are over,
And all the season of snows and sins;
The days dividing lover and lover,
The light that loses, the night that wins;
And time remembered is grief forgotten
And frosts are slain and flowers begotten,
And in green underwood and cover
Blossom by blossom the spring begins.

—Algernon Charles Swinburne,
Atalanta in Calydon

Introduction

WHAT can be said of death?

After thousands of years, we still grope for comfort and consolation. So many books have been written from every viewpoint. Yet there is no prescription to cure grief nor a preferred solution to the emotional, physical, or spiritual dimensions of death. Grieving varies from person to person.

The approach of this book is different. *You* are the writer. Only *you* can express your moods, your pain, and your search for healing. This is your personal diary to write in when you desire your memories, your disappointments, and your struggles for peace and hope. Keeping a journal will help you to understand your own feelings.

As you recall the pages of the past, take your time to consider your individual chapters for the future. One part of your life has ended. You are now writing your new beginnings.

# GRIEVING

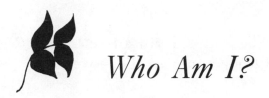

Who Am I?

THE DEATH OF A LOVED ONE brings emotional turmoil for you, the survivor. It requires many adjustments in your life. It is the most stressful of *all* of life's changes. You may look into the mirror and not even recognize the way you now look. Something in you is gone which can never be regained. Your old self-image is shattered. You may lose a sense of who you are as spouse, parent, child, friend.

Now you must slowly and painfully adjust to new realities of changing roles and relationships—how people may treat you and how you view yourself. It is a painful period of redefinement, a search for a new identity.

"When I looked in the mirror, I saw a face I didn't recognize—a tired woman in pain. I cried: My God is that me?"

—a widow, a few months after her husband's death

Look into the mirror. What do you see? What do you want to say or scream back?

 # The Faces of Death

DEATH is separation and pain, anger, and grief. It is the loneliness of anguished hours in which you feel your loss so keenly. It is learning to live without the familiar face and smile of a loved one. How can you survive these long, vacant hours when the longings will not go away?

When people ask, "Where does it hurt?" you want to shout, *"Everywhere."* It's impossible to describe your pain. For death touches your total self: your emotional equilibrium as well as your physical well-being.

It's important to grieve. Grief is love not wanting to let go. You grieve deeply because you loved deeply. Grief is a natural act, a necessary process. To ignore your despair or to postpone it will only intensify your pain at a later time.

Some people may think: "The funeral is over. Everything should be back to normal." But grief does not travel along a straight line and then abruptly fade away or disappear. There are no prescribed stages as if you were going through a series of hoops. The road to recovery is more like a roller coaster. Moods shift erratically, sometimes for the slightest reasons.

It is not unusual for your pain to intensify after six or eight months. Often it will erupt anew after the full cycle of meaningful dates such as birthdays and anniversaries. There is no timetable for grief.

Be patient with yourself. Try not to compare your emotions with others who have suffered similar losses. Don't allow well-intentioned people to orchestrate your feelings with "you must" or "you should." Trust yourself to do what is right for you.

"When my wife died, I felt like I was going through an operation without anesthesia."

—a widower

Many people need to relive through those first trying moments of death. You might wish to write all the details you can recall—the dying process, the funeral, the internment.

You probably never imagined that grief could be so painful. It is a pain like no other pain. Are there times when you feel that you can't make it through another day? Or that you are "losing your mind?" What helps you to "survive" these agonizing periods?

Shock

You hear the words of loss; yet, you don't understand what is being said. Suddenly, the world appears so unreal. You feel like you are in a trance reacting automatically and mechanically. It is as if your body is disassociated from your mind. You can't concentrate; you are disorganized and disoriented. It is not unusual to be more accident-prone.

Feelings of shock usually last a few days to a few weeks. Numbness insulates you from the world of reality. Don't be surprised if a terrible let-down comes later on. The mourning process is just beginning.

"I look at all the cars. Then for some reason I start to count them—the way I did as a child when our family went on a long trip and I wanted to make the time disappear . . . But then I realize the cars I'm counting are funeral cars. The people inside these cars are crying for my child. My child is dead!"

—a bereaved parent

Your initial feeling may be numbness. When did you begin to realize that the death was real? What did you say or do?

15

Denial

"I can't believe it."

"I won't believe it."

"I don't believe it."

"It's a bad dream. When I wake up, I'll find that it really didn't happen."

You may see the name in the obituary and fantasize that it's a coincidence, just another person with the exact same name as your loved one. The telephone rings and you hope against hope that your beloved will call. You set an extra plate on the table. Secretly, you may think or pretend that your loved one is still alive. You want to hold on to the past so life will go on just as before.

Denial is usually temporary. You simply need more time. It's your way of saying, "I don't want to think about it." Disbelief is your attempt to avoid the necessary process of suffering.

"Neither the sun nor death
can be looked at
with a steady eye."
    —La Rochefoucauld

*It is natural to close your eyes to that which is painful.
There are still probably moments when you can't believe
your loved one has died. Write about these times.*

Guilt

Few survivors escape without some feelings of guilt and regret.

"If only I
made him/her go to the doctor sooner."
had not let my son/daughter take the car that night."
had gone to a better hospital."
had not left the bedroom for a cup of coffee and had been there when it happened."
could do it all over again."
"I should have
been more understanding."
been more loving and affectionate."
acted differently."

Death almost always involves "if onlys" and "I should haves." You may search out in your heart for ways you think you failed your beloved. It is a quest for another chance. It's as if you need to atone for your "sins" by punishing yourself.

But there is enough pain already. All relationships have difficult moments. Feelings of regret are normal. But continual self-recrimination denies what you are— a fallible human being who usually does your best under trying circumstances. Blaming yourself will not bring your loved one back to life. All you can do is to avoid in the future what you regret in the past. Most of all, try to forgive yourself for being human.

"My mother was in such pain. I remember sitting by her bed praying that she would die. How can I ever forgive myself for that?"

—a middle-aged person's reaction to a parent's death

Death can bring so many regrets. What do you wish you had done differently? How would that have helped you now?

_____

_____

_____

_____

_____

_____

_____

_____

_____

_____

_____

Anger

You may feel a bitterness that lingers for a long time:

"I don't deserve this!"
"Why me?"
'Why my beloved?"

Fury is difficult to contain. You may blame the doctors, the nurses, the hospital, the clergy, the funeral director, friends, God—even your loved one for leaving you alone and bereft. Making others responsible for the loss could be a way of exonerating yourself.

Resentment is a natural part of the grief process and helps you to express your anguish and frustration at the curtailment of a life so precious. Bottling up anger causes more stress and can lead to depression.

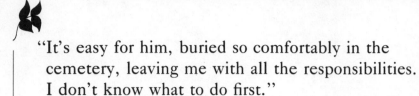

"It's easy for him, buried so comfortably in the cemetery, leaving me with all the responsibilities. I don't know what to do first."

—a widow

It is normal to be angry when part of your life has died. A sense of helplessness may turn to bitterness. When do you feel most angry? How do you express your emotions? How do your friends and family respond to your resentment? What helps you to work through these feelings?

_____

_____

_____

_____

_____

_____

_____

_____

_____

Tears

"Sometimes I cry for the smallest things. Am I losing my mind?"

You have every reason to cry. Grief is expressed not only in words but tears. Weeping helps you to realize powerful emotions by letting the hurt run out through tears. Crying is not a sign of weakness, nor is it self-pity. Abraham wept, as did the matriarch Rachel. So did Jesus.

Tears are healthy ways of coping and acting out grief—your frustrations, anger, loneliness, and the realization of your agonizing loss. Everyone needs an outlet to discharge pent-up emotions.

Don't take pride in stoicism or self-control.

"The healing began when a friend embraced me, leaving some of his tears on my cheek."

—a clergyperson who was comforted after the stillbirth of his child.

Spontaneous tears may come at unexpected times—like seeing a happy family on television or hearing a familiar song on the radio. What makes you feel like crying? What happens when you hold yourself back? When and where are you able to release these feelings? How do others react to you? How do you wish they would respond?

31

Physical Reactions

The body reacts to the death of a loved one just as does the mind and spirit. Grief may involve such responses as:

sleep disturbances

difficulty in breathing

a tightness in the throat or chest

low energy level

sudden weight loss or gain

headaches and backaches

susceptibility to respiratory upsets, constant colds, and sore throats

dizziness, blurred vision.

Each of the symptoms may occur alone or in any combination or degree of intensity. These are your body's responses to your mental turmoil. Your pain is real; it is not imagined.

Try to do all in your power to maintain your best state of wellness. At this stressful time you are most vulnerable to illness. It is important to have a regular check-up with a competent, understanding physician, to find needed rest, and to have a balanced diet with appropriate exercise. *Neglecting your health will not bring honor to the memory of your loved one.*

"I collapse in bed, but I cannot sleep. My mind races. I feel like there's a jagged rock pressing against my ribs. It's so hard to breathe. After I sleep, I wake up exhausted."

> —a wife after her husband was killed
> in a fatal accident

Your grief touches your body as well as your heart. Since your loved one died, are there physical problems that you have encountered? What are you doing about them? If you are not taking care of yourself, why?

_____

_____

_____

_____

_____

_____

_____

_____

_____

Depression

"My loved one died."
"My life is over, too."
"Nothing matters anymore, nothing."
"Why couldn't it be me instead?"

You may be panicky, out-of-control, feeling that you are sinking lower, lower, lower. Your mind is a jumble; so is your body. The slightest effort leaves you limp. All efforts seem so futile. You want to hide, to shelter yourself from people and activities. You feel alone, naked, unprotected, empty.

"Maybe I am losing my mind," you think. Especially when you may do strange things like getting lost on familiar streets, wandering aimlessly around the house, hearing the voice of your loved one, seeing the person in your dreams, constantly daydreaming about the way things used to be. Know you are not "crazy." These feelings are not uncommon. You are emotionally depleted. Death has wounded you.

Mind-altering tranquilizers and sleeping pills do not eliminate grief. They only interfere with your body and mind's healthy way of coping with the terrible reality of your loss. Drugs suppress constructive emotions of sadness, hostility, and grief. If you bury these necessary feelings, they will surface destructively later on. There are no "shortcuts" to the grieving process. Grief is hell!

"You lied who told me time would ease my pain."
　　　　　　　　　—Edna St. Vincent Millay

With loss, there is a sense of frustration and melancholy. When are you most depressed? What triggers these feelings?

_____

_____

_____

_____

_____

_____

_____

_____

_____

_____

_____

WORKING THROUGH GRIEF

Practical Matters: Day-to-Day Activities

YOU FEEL helpless and powerless to control the events of your life, and yet you are swept along in a rapid tide of activities. How can you meet these responsibilities when it's so difficult to summon up the energy to get up in the morning or even decide what to eat for breakfast? Yet, you must attend to practical matters.

Set attainable goals for yourself. It can be as simple as writing a few acknowledgment cards each day. You will feel so much better after you complete these few tasks and you start to take charge of your life.

Seek good advice from a trusted, competent friend, relative, or financial advisor. Problems will not abruptly disappear. Keep a list of things that need immediate attention. Postpone major decisions if you can. Wait before changing your job or deciding to sell your house. Judgments are too uncertain when you are just confronted with the suffering of death.

"When my husband died, I just wanted someone to put their arms around me and take care of me the way my mother used to when I was sick. But now my kids were looking to me to take care of them. I felt so alone. I kept thinking: 'How am I even going to get by?' And then there were the taxes to be done, the bills, the house . . . I was overwhelmed."

—a widow

It's difficult enough to go through the loss of a loved one. Yet there are important matters that you must attend to. Make a list of the practical details that must soon be fulfilled.

_____

_____

_____

_____

_____

_____

_____

_____

Special Dates and Holidays

THERE ARE significant days that are especially difficult: birthdays, anniversaries, Mother's Day, Father's Day, Thanksgiving, Christmas, Chanukah, New Year's Eve, Passover, Easter, Bar and Bat Mitzvahs, weddings, confirmations. At one time in your life they were such joyful, sharing family times. Now these days can be times of wrenching memories, lost hopes and dreams. How can you survive these particular days when you feel such pain and sadness, so empty and abandoned, angry and depressed?

Your loved one is always missed, but never more than on these special days. Your stomach may be knotted at the prospect of dealing with certain dates. There are no magic formulas to remove the dread, your fears, your anxieties.

You may, however, ease your grief by planning ahead. Leave nothing to chance. Expectations should be realistic. It's probably going to be a "tough" day. Decide what you think you can handle most comfortably. Make your needs known in advance to your family, friends, and relatives.

Pace yourself both in preparation for the day and the manner you will commemorate it. It is not necessary for you to assume total responsibility for the family dinner or "holiday" party. You might ask someone to help you or allow that person to start a new tradition in a different home. Try to be with the people who will allow you to convey your thoughts freely, and permit you to cry and laugh with them as well. If family or friends are not available, determine if a support group has activities for that special day. *Do what is best for you.*

You might change the routine by alternating the usual rituals—such as the time for the family meal or when you traditionally open gifts. You could buy tickets to the theatre for yourself and a special friend who has been helpful through your period of bereavement. If you feel the need or desire, you might spend some time on this special day by yourself in meditation or prayer, or on a quiet walk. You may need time alone to be in touch with your memories.

Be flexible. Whatever you choose one particular year could be modified the next—like going away the following year for a vacation. After the special day, evaluate what you think you can do more meaningfully in the future. Growth and change go hand in hand.

If you are able, don't be reluctant to try to enjoy parts of the day even with its intense painful recollections. Memories of yesterdays are important but don't let them take the beauty out of today. It may help to know that those who have lived through these special days have often remarked that anticipation was frequently worse than the day itself.

"My son always sat between me and my father at Thanksgiving—the three generations together. But this year, I sat next to my father. It was as if no chair or person ever existed. Not one person mentioned my child's name. Unbelievable—like he never lived!"

—a bereaved parent

Just when you may think that you are feeling a little bit better, a special day brings back such agonizing memories. What do you remember most clearly about celebrating the date when your loved one was alive? What could help to lighten the burden for next year's special day?

_____

_____

_____

_____

_____

_____

_____

_____

Children Need Help, Too

DEATH IS a crisis which is shared by *all* members of the family. Children are often forgotten. The adults' silence and secrecy deprive children of the opportunity of expressing their own sorrow. When you overlook the youngsters' suffering, you heighten their sense of isolation and make more difficult their adjustment to their loss.

Help your children cope with their feelings. Be gentle with them. Respond according to each one's age, temperament, intellectual and emotional capabilities, and, of course, the particular relationship to the one who died. Give tender, straightforward explanations. Ask if they have any questions. Try to give them words for their questions. Hear not only their words but also be attentive to their hidden nonverbal communications—such as hostile behavior, prolonged withdrawal, or lack of interest in school and friends. Let them know that they need not hide their true feelings, fears, and fantasies.

Most of all, stay close to them. Hug them. Let them feel your warmth and affection. Be available when they need to talk. What is most essential is to provide them with special amounts of attention, praise, and emotional support. Grief is a family experience.

"Until my father told me how angry he felt about my mother's death, I thought he was mad at me."

—a ten-year-old

It is so hard to reach out to your children when you are in such pain, to offer support when you can hardly support yourself. Nevertheless, children need your help when they are in crisis. How did you tell each child about the death? What were the individual responses? What was most difficult in discussing the loss with them? How do you help each other?

 SUPPORT

Friends

YOU ALONE can make it, but you cannot make it alone. You need to share your feelings with someone you trust, who will not judge you but accept you where you are. You need to give expressions of your loneliness, bitterness, fears, love, and maybe even a sense of relief.

Hopefully, you will have friends who will lend a sympathetic ear and comfort you. They will keep in touch after the funeral, invite you to their homes, and be there for you. They will allow you your privacy when you need it and not attempt to overpower you. You will *never* forget their kindnesses. Thank them for caring.

However, don't expect your friends to understand you unless you communicate your needs and feelings clearly. They can't read your mind. Do not try to protect them by silence. If you repeatedly say that "I'm fine," how could they know that you're in need of their help? You must signal when you want their companionship and assistance.

Unfortunately, there may be some friends who will disappoint you. They may simply not know how to deal with individuals in grief. They may be frightened by the death of your loved one as a reminder that their own beloved will also die. They might even think that they are actually helping when they provide easy platitudes that wound you:

"I know your child died, but you have other youngsters."

"I hear that there's a lot of new research being done now. It won't take long before they find a cure for the disease that killed your wife."

"You're young enough, you'll have another child."

"At least he died quickly."

"You'll feel like your old self in no time."

These people cannot possibly know what you are feeling. It does not help to argue with them. You now know that you cannot expect them to be tuned to your special needs. You may simply have to look inside yourself for help and develop your own resources as well as new friendships.

It's a difficult time for your friends, too. They are at a different place in life and do not understand you. After all, during these turbulent times, you don't always understand yourself, do you? Forgive them.

"When I ask you to listen to me and you start giving me advice, you have not done what I asked.

When I ask you to listen to me and you begin to tell me why I shouldn't feel that way, you are trampling on my feelings.

When I ask you to listen to me and you feel you have to do something to solve my problems, you have failed me, strange as that may seem.

Listen! All I asked was that you listen, not talk or do—just hear me."

—author unknown

Death brings many surprises. Some friends—whom you counted on—were conspicuous by their absence. When they did appear, they made statements that hurt you. On the other hand, it may be surprising that casual acquaintances may have filled in the breach and helped you through your despair. Are your relationships with your friends changing? How are they helping you through your ordeal? How are you coping with those friends who "let you down?"

_____

_____

_____

_____

_____

 *Self Help Groups*

FRIENDS AND FAMILY may not always be able to offer all the support you need. They are involved with their own families and problems of life which are now so different from yours. Even though they want to help, they may be uncomfortable by the death of your loved one.

But grief-companions in support groups have been through the valley of the shadow of death. They understand the value of talking and crying together and searching for other alternatives to reinvesting in life. Linking up with others who have experienced similar losses could provide the emotional assistance in working through your own fears and frustrations. You learn how to be more patient and *more loving* with yourself, your family, your friends. People in similar situations often become second families to each other, reaching out of isolation to a meaningful support system. Just remember, everyone needs help. Don't be afraid to ask—and to accept help when given.

Some national self-help groups to consider are found at the back of the book. For local groups, contact the national organizations, your clergy, funeral director, or mental health association.

"It's sometimes hard being with my old friends. I feel I'm a burden to them, like I'm a fifth wheel. But in my widow/widower group, I belong and I am no longer alone."

—a widow/widower member

Many have eased their pain by being able to talk to or listen to other bereaved. It may take a lot of courage to attend that first meeting. Yet, know that you will not be an unwelcome guest. The other members have had their hearts broken, too. Together you may offer each other support. If you have attended a self-help group, what were your reactions? How were the members like you or different? If you haven't attended, what do you imagine a meeting to be like?

Helping Others

As YOU WORK through your grief, you may find some degree of fulfillment in helping others as well. The experience of suffering creates the ability to assist other sufferers. After all, you are the real expert in understanding tribulation and pain. The ability to help the hurt comes more easily to those who have known hurt. Your experience is now placed at the service of others. You have turned your grief into creative energy. *As you counsel others, you gain insights into yourself.*

Life goes on—even with suffering. There are new opportunities for social contact, new friends. Your mind is more actively engaged. Helping to carry someone else's load is guaranteed to lighten your own. You are needed and wanted, less alone and lonely. By your helpfulness and kindness, you bring honor to the memory of your beloved.

"If I can stop one heart
from breaking,
I shall not live in vain;
If I can ease one life
the aching,
Or cool one pain,
Or help one fainting robin
Unto his nest again,
I shall not live in vain."
　　　　—Emily Dickinson

It may be difficult to reach out when you're in such agony. Think about someone you know who has suffered a similar death in the family. Write a detailed letter to this person, sharing some of the real feelings involved, the problems to be alerted to, and the means that have helped you to cope more effectively.

_____

_____

_____

_____

_____

_____

_____

Religion

MORE THAN any other of the life-cycle events, the death of a loved one raises the most profound spiritual issues about good and evil, reward and punishment, and a concept of an afterlife.

Religious faith helps many in finding comfort in spirituality. There are the Holy scriptures, meaningful rituals, and community support. Your theology might aid you to release those aching feelings of helplessness and guilt and to make some sense of death and life.

For others, the painful loss shakes up beliefs. "What kind of God would allow this to happen?" You may feel abandoned, forsaken, cheated by God. Many spiritual leaders in history have reacted this very way. The questioning of faith is a normal expression of anguish and consistent with later spiritual growth. As time goes along, you may eventually draw strength from your religious heritage and find that you are not so angry with God after all. Faith may not take away heartache but faith can help you to live with it better, to accept the unacceptable.

Some of the following readings have sustained mourners throughout the centuries:

The Lord is my shepherd, I shall not want;
He maketh me to lie down in green pastures.
He leadeth me beside the still waters!
He restoreth my soul.
He guideth me in straight paths for His name's sake.
Yea, though I walk through the valley of the shadow
    of death,
I will fear no evil; for Thou art with me.
Thy rod and Thy staff, they comfort me.
Thou preparest a table before me in the presence
    of mine enemies;
Thou has annointed my head with oil, my cup
    runneth over.
Surely goodness and mercy shall follow me all the
    days of my life;
And I shall dwell in the house of the Lord forever.
                                              —Psalm 23

There is an appointed time for everything,
    and a time for every affair under the heavens.
A time to be born, and a time to die;
    a time to plant, and a time to uproot the plant.
A time to weep, and a time to laugh;
    a time to mourn, and a time to dance;
A time to keep, and a time to cast away.
                        —Qoheleth (Ecclesiastes) 3:1-3, 4

You can trust God
not to let you be tried beyond your strength,
and with any trial He will give you a way out of it
and the strength to bear it.
                                    —Corinthians II: 3

Lord, make me an instrument of your peace.
Where there is hatred, let me sow love;
Where there is injury, pardon.
Where there is doubt, faith;
Where there is despair, hope.
Where there is darkness, light;
and where there is sadness, joy.
Lord, make me not so much want to be comforted
as to comfort, to be loved as to love.
For it is in giving that we receive,
in pardoning that we are pardoned and
in dying we are born to eternal life.

—Prayer of St. Francis

God grant me the serenity
   to accept the things I cannot change,
The courage to change the things I can,
   and the wisdom to know the difference.

—author unknown

"It was comforting to find that when my faith in myself was running low, I could turn to another faith which had stood the test of thousands of years. If that faith and the people who trusted in it could survive, then so could I."

—a young physician after his wife's suicide

Have your feelings about religion changed since the death of your loved one? Do the words of the Psalmist reflect your own thoughts: "My God, my God, why have you forsaken me?" (22:1). Has your faith helped you to find strength and solace? How has your clergyperson responded to your needs? You might want to write down some of the inspirational passages that bring comfort to you.

_____

_____

_____

_____

_____

_____

_____

_____

RECOVERY

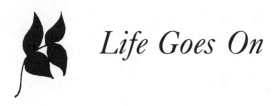

Life Goes On

"MY LOVED ONE is dead. I'm in pain. But I'm alive. And now I must pick up the pieces."

Recovery does not come automatically. It takes a great deal of time and unremitting effort. Emotional scars will remain. But accepting hardship is the first pathway through your pain. Time alone does not heal grief. You must confront your suffering head on. Work through your grief *day by day*, one lightened step at a time. Otherwise the future can be overwhelming.

There will be better moments for you. The "down" times will return again but you will notice they don't remain as long as when your loved one died. It's all right to begin healing. Feeling better is not an indication that you loved less. Rather it is a sign of your determination to affirm life despite its bitterness and tribulations.

"In three words, I can sum
up everything I've learned
about life. *It goes on.*
Despite our fears and worries
life continues."

—Robert Frost

*A poet once said: "Life goes on. I know not why"
(Edna St. Vincent Millay). The loved one has died but
you are here. What is the hardest part of going on
living?*

_____

_____

_____

_____

_____

_____

_____

_____

 *Growing Through Loss*

SOME DAY you will not ask as many *whys:* "Why?" Why me?" "Why did it happen?"

You will begin to understand that there are no complete answers to the questions of *why?* One day you will begin to ask a different question: *"How* do I gain some control over my life?" You will want to rediscover yourself. Only *you* can do it.

The road to recovery is now your foremost challenge. You will need to understand more about yourself in order to gain new perspectives and uncover your inner resources. You will allow yourself to make mistakes, to explore your feelings, and to come to terms with your grief. You're at the crossroads of life—formulating new directions.

Through these trials of confrontation, you will begin to grow, enlarge your goals, refine your needs, and redefine your future. As your outlook in life changes, so will your self-image. You realize that you are not the same person who once felt that you could never survive. As Benjamin Franklin said: "Those things that hurt, instruct."

"Since my child died, I have changed. I don't put off things we can do together as a family. I may never have another chance. Knowing love and adjusting to loss has made me a more loving and caring person."

—bereaved parent

You are a different person from when your loved one was still alive. There has been so much agony. At the same time there has been growth. Not because you wanted your life this way but because of the changes you have had to make to adjust to your great loss. Write a letter to yourself. Tell of the new insights you have gained. Give yourself credit for your courage, strength, and fortitude.

Time Remembered

WHEN CHERISHED ties are broken, the chain of love is shattered. Yet, even in pain you are beginning to realize that your beloved will never vanish as long as beloved thoughts remain within you. No one can take away your hurt because no one can take away your love. Nothing can detract from the happiness you once shared. Memory is a master painter—lining indelible images upon your mind's canvas with reminiscences both happy and sad.

As long as you live, so will your loved one. Memories bring strength and blessings. The beauty of that life is forever enshrined in your heart, abiding as a lasting and loving benediction in the unending cycle of time.

"It was a few months after my grandmother's death that I was taking a course in creative writing. My teacher suggested that I record some of my thoughts to help me work through my sadness. This diary became my memorial to her. Even now I read aloud the pages. I still laugh and cry about times we shared together."

—a young adult

Though time and space separate you from your beloved, the bridge of memories helps to span the distance.

Use these blank pages to record those special memories that help to sustain you during these difficult periods. You might also write down some of the statements from letters of condolence that are precious to you.

Endings and Beginnings

THE ACT of giving up someone so dear is excruciating. But, to grow you now have to "let go." Otherwise you become stuck in a history that can never again be repeated. To live only in the past will only create more misery and loneliness. "Letting go" means finding out that there is something in you beside fear, anger, unhappiness, and frustration.

It's a risk to attempt new beginnings. But hasn't life always been a risk? To cry is to risk appearing weak. To laugh is to risk appearing foolish. To reach out is to risk entanglement. To go forward is to risk failure. Yet, the greater risk is for you to risk nothing. For there will be *no* further possibilities of learning and changing, of traveling upon the journey of life.

You still do not like what has happened in your life. You still do not understand *why*. But you're still you— groping for new paths to trod. You were strong to hold on. *You will be stronger to go forward to new beginnings.*

"As the scars begin to heal, I feel like a tree covering itself with new growth. The world sings a broken song. My loved one is dead. But I'm alive. It's time to start living again."

> —reflections following the anniversary of a death

However long and dark the night, the dawn is sure to break. Look into the mirror again. How do you think you have changed since the death of your loved one? What new goals are you setting for yourself—one month from now, and one year from now, and how can they best be achieved? Congratulate yourself on your survival and progress.

_____

_____

_____

_____

_____

_____

_____

_____

 # A Sanskrit Proverb

Look to this day, for it is life.
For yesterday is already a dream
and tomorrow is only a vision.
But today well lived makes
every yesterday
a dream of happiness, and
every tomorrow
a vision of hope.

Afterword

THIS IS your journal. Keep it in a convenient place. Continue to use it as your personal diary to record your survival through your terrible loss.

Months and even years later, reread what you have written. Hopefully you will be able to look back and say: "I've done it. I made it from despair to where I am today. I've gone on living."

APPENDIXES

Personal Information

You have been through such a terrible loss. And yet there may be practical details that demand your attention. The following checklists may prove helpful for your welfare and protection.

Important People and Places

Attorney _____

Address _____

Town/City _____

Telephone _____

Clergy _____

Address _____

Town/City _____

Telephone _____

Funeral Director _____

Address _____

Town/City _____

Telephone _____

Cemetery Representative _____

Address _____

Town/City _____

Telephone _____

Physician _____

Address _____

Town/City _____

Telephone _____

Tax Consultant _____

Address _____

Town/City _____

Telephone _____

Executor of Will _____

Address _____

Town/City _____

Telephone _____

Bank Officer _____

Address _____

Town/City _____

Telephone _____

100

Stockbroker _____

Address _____

Town/City _____

Telephone _____

Employer _____

Address _____

Town/City _____

Telephone _____

Fraternal Order/Professional Group Leader _____

Address _____

Town/City _____

Telephone _____

Insurance Agent _____

Address _____

Town/City _____

Telephone _____

Social Security Representative _____

Office Address _____

City/Town _____

Telephone _____

Your Social Security Number _____

Social Security Number of your loved one _____

Veterans Administrative Office _____

Address _____

City/Town _____

Telephone _____

Death Payment

In practically all cases where the deceased is covered by Social Security, there is a single payment that is made.

Survivor Benefits

Monthly benefits may be payable to certain dependents and survivors.

Medicare Benefits

Medicare benefits are frequently available to help pay final medical bills if the deceased qualifies under the provisions of this medical insurance coverage.

Veterans Administration payments are offered to the surviving family of qualified veterans.

Vital Material

Document	Number and Location
Will	_____
Safe Deposit Key and Box	_____
Bankbook(s)	_____
	_____
Checkbook(s)	_____
Insurance Policies	_____
Stocks and Bonds	_____
Real Estate Holdings	_____
Deed(s) to property:	_____
Bill(s) of sale	_____
Mortgages, Personal Notes:	_____
Accounts Receivables	_____
Income Tax Returns	_____
Tax Receipts	_____
Veteran's Discharge Certificate	_____
Cemetery Lot Certificate	_____

Acknowledgment Letters

For expressions of sympathy, flowers, contributions, love

Name _____

Address _____

City/Town _____

Name _____

Address _____

City/Town _____

Name _____

Address _____

City/Town _____

Name _____

Address _____

City/Town _____

104

Name _____

Address _____

City/Town _____

Name _____

Address _____

City/Town _____

Name _____

Address _____

City/Town _____

Name _____

Address _____

City/Town _____

Name _____

Address _____

City/Town _____

Name _____

Address _____

City/Town _____

Name _____

Address _____

City/Town _____

Name _____

Address _____

City/Town _____

Name _____

Address _____

City/Town _____

Name _____

Address _____

City/Town _____

Personal Mementos

You and many other people have treasured your loved one. During this time of sorrow you probably have felt touched by expressions of love from other friends and relatives of the beloved. You may find that you want to present these special people with personal items that belonged to your loved one, so that others may share your remembrances.

Recipient   *Item*

_____   _____

_____   _____

_____   _____

_____   _____

_____

_____   _____

_____   _____

_____   _____

_____   _____

_____   _____

Personal Thoughts

113